I hate you, I miss you, it's confusing

Mary Bryant

BookLeaf Publishing

Presentation by *BookLeaf Publishing*

Web: www.bookleafpub.com

E-mail: info@bookleafpub.com

ISBN: 978-93-5761-082-7

First edition 2022

DEDICATION

To Brother, Joseph Gerald Moncrief.

You continue to elicit the same frustrations in
death as in life, but I miss you terribly and wish
we had more time together. Love always, Sister

ACKNOWLEDGEMENT

To my parents, thank you for the little brother. I know at one time I wished the gypsies would take him, but it turns out I really did become quite fond of him. Love Baby Girl.

To my Dear Husband, you have been through it all with me thus far. I appreciate how you remain a rock and a source of positivity when I get into a grief tailspin. Plus, you remind me there are still good times to be had and that I choose what memories to dwell upon.

To friends who bore witness to the good, bad, and ugly parts of my relationship with my brother, your ability to listen without judgement and pray without ceasing over the years is a gift I cherished.

To friends who kept a hand on my back to hold me up on this journey, thank you for reminding me it's acceptable to be the one who needs help and not always the one giving it. The cards, letters, texts, flowers, books, meals, errands, and hugs were a lifeline. You are gems.

To all those who I have met that experienced loss of sibling, I am grateful for your experience, strength, and hope that you so freely share. Although it is a club we did not want to join, it is comforting to be in presence of people who understand without need for words. Perhaps we will work to find another common bond we can share other than our loss. You are the strongest people I know.

Who?

Who will help me now
Deal with family issues
No one knows like you

Prankster

2

Fake teeth, mullet wig
Always in mood for a prank
You made your own fun

Dad Joy

The love of his life
brown-eyed sassy little girl
Who brought him so much joy

Fatherhood 1

4

Fatherhood changed him
Catalyst for a clean life
Becoming better

Fatherhood 2

Fighting for your right
To be a caring parent
You never gave up

Holiday Hell

Your Christmas with her
Gas station receipt for proof
Heartbreak of no show

Sister

I may fail all things
But I was always the best
Sister so he said

Sickness 1

Thin gaunt defeated
Your inner light diminished
A shell of your self

Donald

Grabbed by the collar
Pushed into a better life
By non-blood brother

Pushers for Profit

Sackler family
The ultimate drug pushers
What is one life worth?

Silence

The silent treatment
Always signaled a dark spell
Come back brother dear

Gum Anyone

Chewing gum fiercely
Anxiety was channeled
Trident melon mint

Full Bucket

13

The amount of love
Our parents poured into you
Fills the world's buckets

Pick a Partner

14

Your picker was broke
Choosing life partners was not
A skill you possessed

Missing

15

When my head is still
And my heart connects to it
I miss you the most

Boy Toys

Penny racer cars
Dirty Tonka trucks at play
Little brother toys

Sickness 2

17

Addiction grips you
Bad decisions burden you
Depression sets in

The Disguise

Life of the party
Wild, free and very foolish
Hiding your unease

Seat Mate

19

Wheels up Brother said
Only one flight together
Thought there would be more

Family Trip

Disney World at last
Backpacks and walkie-talkies
Inside jokes for life

Joe

21

A heart for others
Always wrestling with himself
To be right, do right